THE SILENCING OF HIM

Written by Jason White

Published by HG Publishing
First Edition

JASON WHITE

lives in Barrie, Ontario, Canada doing what he loves most: creating, and being a father. Jason is the father of five and grandfather of four.

Jason enjoys volunteering in many capacities, and writing or creating in his wood shop or kitchen. Whatever he is doing, he likes to do it with his family.

If you've enjoyed this book or any other book published by Jason White, or HG Publishing, please consider leaving an honest review. All reviews help the author reach more readers.

Other Books Available
On Amazon

Passion
She
About Face
Reaching
Journey Home
Sleep: Evergreen Edition – Seasons Collection
Ransom Notes: A Macabre Hypothesis
Reflections: not so subtle words
Resurrect: So Below Edition – Seasons Collection
Healing
Reality
An Angrier Man
The Diary of a Warrior
LOVElier Days
The Way Aliens Take Over
The Patreon Files: Volume 1
Things I May Say – From Time-to-Time
The Fools Journey
Beautiful Disaster
Fucking Our Way to Freedom
Shattered
Monsters In My Closet
A Crazier Man
My Public Downfall
Sickness
Filled with Magic
When Death Comes on a Tuesday
Imposter Syndrome
Chaos Reigns
All That Was Left Unsaid
Changes
In The Beginning: Anthology
Live: Warm Summer Breeze Edition – Seasons Collection
You're the One
Transitioning to Freedom

He'd look at his father and beg for a new life;
for the beatings to end,
for someone who would simply hug him.

Sometimes he'd look at the man he called dad
with admiration and unconditional love.
Because, after-all, that is what children naturally do.

Yet, most days, his love and admiration turned to fear
and the fear to despair
because he didn't know real value in anything else.

He was learning to hate himself,
to quiet his voice.
He was learning he had no value at all.

JASON WHITE

THE SILENCING OF HIM

His voice is stolen from him at a young age.
Man up.
Come on, big boys don't cry.
Be strong, shake it off.
Stand up, be a man.
Don't show emotion.
Knock him out if he does that again.
Isn't that cute, he must like her.
Boys will be boys.
Etcetera, and all that other shit.

It is simple to them,
now isn't it?
The problems they create
are someone else's, after-all.
Someone else's,
but mostly his
when he can't connect with anyone
ever.

When he tried to speak
nothing ever came out.
He was misaligned and broken,
and was never put back quite right.
Rather, he was never given a chance
so he stayed broken,
stayed misaligned.
Trying to put himself back together
for the rest of his days.

Like the Man in the Iron Mask
he is made to be faceless,
his voice muted by years of no use.
His rancid memories
of being patted on the head
and told to run along and play.
Better to be seen than to be heard
and better yet, not to be seen at all.

It's okay,
I was only kidding around.

Don't take things too seriously.
You're always taking things too seriously.

He attempts to set a boundary,
like it is his human right to do.
They constantly reiterate how wrong he is.
Boundaries can only be set
when it makes the others comfortable.

Every time he tries to speak
he laughs at himself,
at the person he wants to be.
Every time he tries to speak
he betrays himself
with the words they want to hear.

He's always smiling,
always laughing.
He was so easy to talk to.
He was such a fun guy.
Those are the things that they'd say
before they proceeded with
I don't understand
why he'd end his life.

He barely knows the difference
between fact or fiction.
He finds it hard to differentiate
between truth and lie.
He is so entangled in the web,
he will never untangle from it.

The way he'd look at his guardian angel
as if to say,
please take me away from this place.
Please cleanse my life of this dis-ease.
Please take all my memories.
Please, I beg of you, let me begin anew.

Mommy fell to the floor,
high as fuck.
another moment when he lost his voice.
He looked around
waiting for a loving hand.
Nobody came.
They just left her there on the floor,
they just left him where he stood.

The more people who show him that trust is an illusion, the more he silences himself to suit them.

Fractured bones,
fractured skulls,
fractured voices,
fractured souls.

Opportunity lost
to become whole.

Now and again
he gains the courage to use his voice.
but then
he is torn down, worse than before.
The pain is always hard for him to bear.
The pain becomes worse than before.
He finds it hard to see the point
to use his voice anymore.

Graduating from a boy
to a young man
his voice was left so far behind
he doesn't know where to find it.
He tries to look back
but it's too far gone
and life is moving way too fast.
So he fakes a smile
and fakes a laugh
so that nobody knows
he has lost his voice.

The way she looks at him,
he knows she wants him
to approach her
and say hello.
But as he tries to speak
nothing comes out.
This is his greatest curse.

His social awkwardness
makes him a pretty useless person.
He has never been able to speak out,
he doesn't know himself.
How could he?
A person's voice is the centre to their personage,
and his has been lost,
or rather, never found.
So, he bumbles through life,
always on the verge of tears,
never to know who he is.

He tells a joke
and they snicker at his awkwardness.

He flirts with a pretty girl
and she says he is cute.

He states a problem
and he is told it will be fine.

He shows his feelings
and he is told he is weak.

He becomes angry
and he is told he is too much.

He withdraws
and he is told he is being abusive.

He shuts down,
the words coming from his mouth are shallow
and meaningless.
His fire diminishing to grey ash.

He tells his mom that she's pretty
and she tells him he doesn't know what he says.

He tells his dad he is handsome
and he tells him to go play.

Don't worry about it.
It's okay.
It's fine.
You're being controlling.
You're too serious.
You're being a buzz kill.
Way to suck the joy out of life.
You're neurotic.
You're ... silenced.

It's none of your business
is a funny statement.
Sometimes it's true
and sometimes it is used to silence.

I would have liked to go to France
but somebody else put their hand up first,
every single day,
and I was always looked over
as a result.

He looked at me
always sad,
always feeling alone.
He said to me
nice guys finish last,
so I became a jerk.
But that's not really what he meant either,
now is it?
But then I was stuck
because I didn't know how to ask for help.

He opened himself completely
to the ones he thought were friends.
but then everything he told them
was repeated to someone else.

Beautiful sentiments
like I Love You
and Great Job
can be used to silence too.

The alcoholic ragers
taught him that words are vapid

Slacking in every way,
he learns and relearns
that he is powerless.

Moving from youth
into manhood
his voice was left so far behind
he doesn't know where to find it.
He tries to look back
but it's too far gone
and life is moving way too fast.
So he fakes a smile
and fakes a laugh
so that nobody knows
he has lost his voice.

He thought he could trust her,
he began using his voice again
- practicing, building it from nothing.
He allowed her to fool him.
She took it all back, and more.

He faked it
from one job to the next,
faking his confidence.
Only running when
he was about to be found out.

His smile slowly killed him inside
because his smile was fake,
like the rest of him was.
And fakeness leads to toxic
emotional build up.
And that becomes part of who we are
and being toxic is what became familiar,
what he became.

As his family grew
his happiness thinned
because he was showing his children
to be ashamed of their voices.

Life was always more
or less,
let's go with less,
perfect for him

He was born to do great things,
he knew it deep inside.
but they all worked together
to ensure that never happened.

Sometimes a gentle kiss on the cheek
is the weapon of choice
to silence a voice.

Freshly washed sheets.
That is what he is concentrating on,
the freshly washed sheets.
They take him away
to a happier place
as she berates him
for talking too much.
He likes the smell
of freshly washed sheets.
In this happier place
his voice still works
and nobody tries to silence him.

He wanted to be a different man
She would mock him when he spoke
and too when he was silent.
He wanted to be different
for her
for his children
but mostly
for himself
He hated the way she spoke down to him.
And, his children were learning to as well.
His in-laws would snicker
as she dominated him.
He didn't like it.
All he had to do was leave.
But he chose to, instead,
live in a quiet hell.

His mother set the stage
for how he would treat himself -
for who he'd look for
in his life.
His mother set this stage,
then he found someone just like her.
He wanted someone different
but didn't think himself worthy.
He found her
and she convinced him
that he didn't deserve her -
that she was doing him a kindness.
His mother set the stage
then she continued the great work
of tearing him down.

Space and time
are illusive to many.
Yet, to him,
self love and
courage
are important things
that were never known.
He hasn't felt
what it was like
to set a boundary
and have the courage
to see it through.
Instead,
he'd let his boundaries
become trampled,
unrecognizable things.
Simply,
jokes that were attempts
to love himself.
That is what he'd know himself to be,
a joke
and nothing more.
A morbid thought
that would become unbreakable truth
for him.
A truth that would be fortified
by the mixed messages
he'd receive throughout his life.
They'd build him up
with false love
just to poison him along the way.
Setting him up
so they could kick him down -
and, if he dare to speak,
he'd get it twice as hard.

www.ingramcontent.com/pod-product-compliance
Lightning Source LLC
Chambersburg PA
CBHW061703130726

47996CB00006B/2143